Dear Mr. Dickens

Nancy Churnin

illustrated by Bethany Stancliffe

Albert Whitman & Company
Chicago, Illinois

With gratitude for my dear friends, Professor J. Don Vann, Professor Emeritus of the University of North Texas, and his lovely wife, Dolores Vann, for teaching me about Charles Dickens and living Dickens's words: "A loving heart is the truest wisdom"—NC

To my wonderful family and friends—BS

Library of Congress Cataloging-in-Publication data is on file with the publisher.
Text copyright © 2021 by Nancy Churnin
Illustrations copyright © 2021 by Albert Whitman & Company
Illustrations by Bethany Stancliffe
First published in the United States of America in 2021 by Albert Whitman & Company
ISBN 978-0-8075-1530-3 (hardcover)
ISBN 978-0-8075-1529-7 (ebook)
Printed in the United States of America
10 9 8 7 6 5 4 3 JOS 26 25 24 23 22

Design by Aphelandra
Endpaper pattern by Garry Killian/Freepik

For more information about Albert Whitman & Company,
visit our website at www.albertwhitman.com.

*T*hink of someone famous you admire. What would you do if that person said or wrote something unfair?

Would you speak up?

Would you risk getting that person angry?

Eliza Davis did.

Charles Dickens was the most famous writer of Eliza's time. English people from all walks of life eagerly paid two pence for his weekly magazine, *All the Year Round,* to read the latest installments of his stories. Later he'd publish the stories as books that passengers bought at bookshops and railway stations.

But what made Charles Dickens a hero in Eliza's eyes is that he used the power of his pen to help others. When he wrote about children forced to labor in workhouses, people demanded change. When his readers were moved to tears by tales of families struggling in desperate, dirty conditions, they gave what they could to charities. As did Eliza.

Yes, Dickens had a
heart as big as England,
overflowing with
compassion for everyone.

Except...

Eliza remembered when she read Dickens's book *Oliver Twist*, about a poor orphan. She had loved it at first—until she got to Chapter Eight, where she read about the "old shriveled Jew" teaching Oliver to steal.

Eliza was Jewish.

Charles Dickens described "the Jew" as dishonest, selfish, cruel, and ugly. The character's name was Fagin, but over and over Dickens wrote *the Jew, the Jew, the Jew*. Each time, the word hurt like a hammer on Eliza's heart.

England was already a difficult place for Jewish people in the 1860s. Many jobs were closed to them. They didn't have the right to vote or to study or work at universities. If people thought that all Jews were like Fagin, would Jewish people ever be treated fairly?

Someone had to speak up. But who?

Eliza wasn't famous or powerful. But she had the same three things that Charles Dickens had: a pen, paper, and something to say.

She sat down and wrote a letter.

Dear Mr. Dickens,

Eliza dipped her pen in ink. Watching the dark liquid rippling, she hesitated.

Who was she to tell the great man what to say? What if her letter made him write things that were even worse?

But maybe he would change. Didn't lots of people in Dickens's own novels change, like Ebenezer Scrooge?

Eliza's pen scratched her paper. She wrote that Dickens's portrayal of Fagin encouraged "a vile prejudice." She asked him to "atone for a great wrong."

She blotted the ink.

She walked to the postbox, her little son skipping behind.

Would Charles Dickens read her letter? Would he write back?

At his stately house in Kent, Dickens studied the letter that a Mrs. Eliza Davis had sent from London.

A vile prejudice, the letter said.

He frowned as he picked up his pen and began his response.

A little more than two weeks later, Eliza was holding the envelope with the reply from Charles Dickens!

She opened it eagerly. Her hands trembled as she read.

Fagin, Dickens had written sharply, was based on real criminals who were Jewish. There are bad people in the book who are not Jewish too. Atone for a great wrong? Any Jewish people who thought him unfair or unkind—and that included Eliza!—were not "sensible" or "just" or "good tempered," he said.

He might as well have said, "Bah! Humbug!"

Eliza stared at the page. The most famous author of her day, a man known to use his powerful pen for good, didn't like what she had to say! She'd tried and failed. She could cry or...

She sat at her desk. She tapped her foot. Dickens's words moved countless readers to compassion. If only *she* could find the words to move one particular reader.

Scrooge didn't change until after he was visited by the ghosts of the Past, Present, and Future. Eliza's letter summoned those spirits too.

Dear Mr. Dickens...

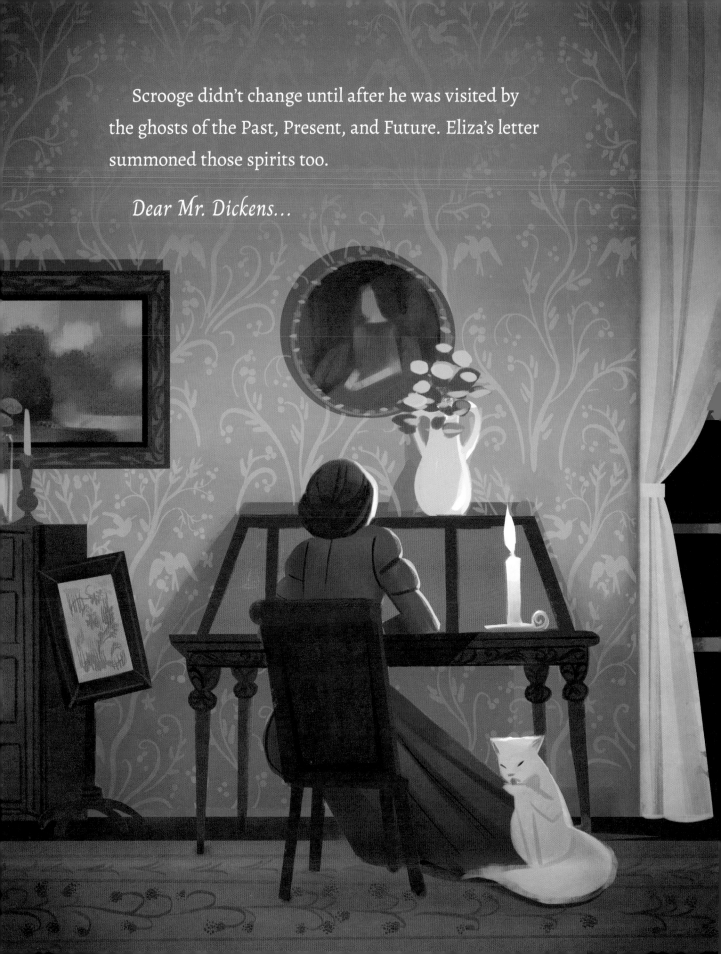

Eliza wrote of Dickens's past, of how he loved Sir Walter Scott's *Ivanhoe* as a boy. Did he remember Scott's great Jewish characters, the noble Isaac of York and his beautiful daughter Rebecca, a skilled healer?

She wrote of Dickens's present. She said that while some of his non-Jewish characters were criminals, *all* his Jewish characters were criminals. That does not present Jewish people "as they really are."

She wrote of Dickens's future. Generations would judge him by how he judged others, including her people, she told him.

She blotted the ink. She'd put everything she had to say in one letter. Would it be too much? Would it be enough?

She slipped it in an envelope. At the postbox, she let her young son mail it.

Months passed with no word from Charles Dickens.
Eliza worried. She heard he was working on a new book.
Was he as angry as he'd been after her first letter?
Would he write characters worse than Fagin?

Finally, chapters of Dickens's novel *Our Mutual Friend* began to appear in monthly installments. Eliza rushed to the newsstand and paid her shillings to read them.

She thumbed through the pages, shaking when she realized he had indeed created another Jewish character.

Had her fears come true?

But no...Mr. Riah was generous and loyal. Dickens named him after the Hebrew word *re'a*, meaning friend. Eliza read the part where Lizzie Hexam, a young woman Mr. Riah helps, says of the Jews:

"I think there cannot be kinder people in the world."

Eliza's eyes filled with tears.

Dear Mr. Dickens...

"[I] thank you very earnestly," Eliza wrote, for "a great compliment paid to myself and to my people."

Dickens wrote back quickly.

"I have received your letter with great pleasure," he said. "And hope to be (as I have always been in my heart) the best of friends with the Jewish people."

And he was. Charles Dickens became, as he'd written of Scrooge, "better than his word. He did it all and infinitely more."

He published essays in his magazine protesting prejudice, including one that addressed how the Jewish people have "too long been wronged by Christian communities."

During *Oliver Twist*'s reprinting, he told the printer to take out many instances of "the Jew" and change them to Fagin, to make it clear that Fagin didn't represent all Jewish people.

A grateful Eliza wrote Dickens one more note—not on paper, but in a copy of an English-Hebrew Bible that she gave him as a gift.

She praised him for having "the noblest quality man can possess," the ability to atone, or make amends for a wrong.

Dickens wrote back one last time.

He was glad she'd spoken up to make things right, he told her.

Eliza was glad she'd spoken up too.

Author's Note

Just before World War II (1939–1945), Great Britain opened its arms to thousands of Jewish refugee children during the Kindertransport. The country had once been one of the most hostile places in Europe for Jewish people, but that had begun to change in the nineteenth century, during the lifetimes of Charles Dickens (1812–1870) and Eliza Davis (1816–1903).

In 1275, King Edward I escalated years of British persecution against Jewish people with the Statutum de Judaismo, a law which decreed that Jews older than seven had to wear a large yellow badge of felt shaped like the tablet of the Ten Commandments on their outer clothing. Jewish people couldn't live among Christians and had to live in restricted areas. They were forbidden to lend money, were unwelcome in trade guilds, and, in 1290, were threatened with expulsion if they didn't convert to Christianity. The only Jews who managed to stay in the country did so by pretending to convert, while worshipping in secret.

It wasn't until 1846, when De Judaismo was repealed, that seeds of inclusion slowly began to flower. In 1858 the Jews Relief Act passed, allowing Jewish people to serve in Parliament. Baron Lionel Nathan de Rothschild, the first Jewish person to sit in the House of Commons, was sworn in without having to declare, as other members of Parliament did, his "true faith as a Christian."

Why did attitudes change? Many deserve credit, including Irish leader Daniel O'Connell, who fought for the repeal of De Judaismo, and Benjamin Disraeli, a Jew who converted to Anglicanism and twice served as a prime minister. But there's no question that the author Charles Dickens also played a key role.

Starting with the success of his first book, *The Pickwick Papers*, in 1836, Dickens was one of the most famous authors in England. Even Queen Victoria was a fan.

Source Notes

All quotes in the book are from the correspondence between Eliza Davis and Charles Dickens, found in *Charles Dickens and His Jewish Characters*, edited by Cumberland Clark (Chiswick Press, 1918), and from Dickens's published works, *Oliver Twist*, *A Christmas Carol*, and *Our Mutual Friend*. Additional information, including the Eliza Davis family tree, courtesy of Frank Gravier, is from "'The Other Woman'—Eliza Davis and Charles Dickens," an article by Murray Baumgarten for *Dickens Quarterly*, Vol. 32, No. 1, pp. 44-70, March 2015.

Mrs. Eliza Davis, courtesy of Hartley Library, University of Southampton

Acknowledgments

I am grateful for the expertise and encouragement of Dickens scholars J. Don Vann, Emeritus Professor at University of North Texas, and his wife, Dolores Vann; Professor Murray Baumgarten, Distinguished Emeritus Professor at UC Santa Cruz, and Founding Director of The Dickens Project; and Professor David Paroissien, Professorial Research Fellow, the University of Buckingham, UK, Emeritus Professor of English, UMass Amherst, and retired longtime editor of *Dickens Quarterly*, the official scholarly publication of the Dickens Society. My thanks, too, to my husband, sons, and family for their love and patience over this book's long, joyful journey.

His work often focused on the social issues of the day: his book *Oliver Twist* inspired readers to support laws to protect children from working in dangerous conditions. But in 1838, when he made Fagin in *Oliver Twist* a criminal and referred to him again and again not by his name, but as "the Jew," it was easy for readers to infer that all Jews were criminals. After Eliza Davis wrote Dickens in 1863 and 1864 to persuade him to create more sympathetic Jewish characters, he began to do so, first in his magazine stories, and then in *Our Mutual Friend*, his last completed novel, published in 1865. That book's portrayal of Mr. Riah, a kind Jewish man, encouraged sympathy for the Jewish community.

Eliza Davis was born in Jamaica around 1816 and moved to England, where she married her cousin, James Phineas Davis, and had ten children. The Davises purchased Dickens's former home, Tavistock House, from the author in 1860. Davis admired Dickens and, like him, cared passionately about helping others. Her first letter to Dickens, in 1863, included a request to support a Jewish charitable endeavor—which he did. She wasn't the first Jewish person to reproach Dickens for his portrayal of Fagin, but it was her sincere care for the underprivileged that changed his heart.

Davis and Dickens exchanged seven letters between June 1863 and March 1867; Davis wrote an eighth letter to Dickens's daughter, Mamie, after his death in 1870. In that letter, Davis praised "the wonderful humanizing effects" of Dickens's "powerful pen" and "the good he has wrought for the present generation." But what meant the most to Davis, she wrote, was Dickens's creation of Riah, which "impressed me thoroughly with the nobility of [Dickens's] character."

Words can change hearts, minds, and history. How fortunate we are that Eliza Davis bravely spoke up for justice and that Charles Dickens listened and used his powerful pen to make his readers listen too.